I0605099

Praise for *SOULMATE AS A VERB*

"*SOULMATE AS A VERB* is the best kind of book: just when you think you know what's coming, Smoot flips the script. Full of wisdom, wry humor, and tenderness, these poems so irresistibly explore the euphoric and the dysphoric, the performance of Black masculinity, and the body as a place and act, as both memory and future. This collection explodes the idea of transition as linear and redefines what we think we know about love. Love, not as a feeling or a noun, but love as an act, love as decision, love as protest, love as in creating each other. It's propulsive, it's unputdownable, it's just so good, and it's going to stay with me for a long, long time."

—Marisa Crane, author of *A Sharp Endless Need*

"*SOULMATE AS A VERB* maps a Black boi's quest to fully inhabit a self, a body, transformed by love and by loss, by the ache of revolution and the ache of depression, by gender as it unfolds against our narrow grids. As such, this searching debut turns relentlessly toward what are, to me, the vital questions: how to "maintain a barrier" enough to maintain one's integrity, yet cultivate enough tenderness to turn toward each other, to change? Though, admittedly, "the heart doesn't take well / to re-arrangement," Kelsey Smoot insists on the poem as "witchcraft," a practice of personal and political transformation, enacting a series of formal experiments in rewriting, unwriting, and imagining elsewise to the heartbreak of the present."

—Cameron Awkward-Rich, author of *An Optimism*

"*SOULMATE AS A VERB* is a cold plunge into the mighty tides of black masculinity's past, present, and daring future; Kelz offers us the shocking opening of his own body as a life raft, an even mightier miracle. through a lush exhibition of rhythm, black family relic, and "fuck it" bravado, he leads us to a more free place, an infinite number of worlds where—whether boi or not or monster or something else entirely—love will be there, and he will always share it. if we need courage to love, then i would boldly say Kelz's work easily marks him as one of the most courageous bois of us all; always a cousin indeed."

—Edwin Bodney, author of *A Study of Hands*

Praise for *SOULMATE AS A VERB*

"*SOULMATE AS A VERB* navigates intimate and communal relationships through the lens of a Black, transmasculine, queer, radical, vulnerable AF speaker. I felt pulled into the music, voice, and lyrical diversity of these poems. Smoot creates a landscape of play, praise, and passion through forms ranging from erasures to golden shovels; their subjects range from Palestine to unrequited love. It devastated and delighted me to experience a poet unafraid to relay the unique experiences of their life while also appealing to the universal desire of wanting a better world—for us and all of our soulmates. I felt seen in this book. Any reader with an open (or broken) heart is sure to find home here."

—KB Brookins, award-winning author of *Pretty: A Memoir*

"This is a blurb of the OG Kelsey L. Smoot who is an alchemist of Black vernacular and a believer in Black people. Proof of that power is in the book you now hold, a volume full of poems about survival inasmuch as adaptation and transition is how any human being must survive. Above all, these are love poems, and often, they are love poems to the self. I envy. I wish I had written as line as strong and leading and direct and slick as, 'i belong to myself these days.'"

—Jericho Brown, author of *The Tradition* and *The New Testament*

SOULMATE AS A VERB

POEMS BY

KELSEY L. SMOOT

Published by DOPAMINE
P.O. Box 363, Joshua Tree, CA 92252
www.dopaminebooks.org

Covert Art: *[we are] being held for the first time*, 2019, by Texas Isaiah.
Layout & Design: Brooke Palmieri

ISBN: 978-1-63590-282-2
Distributed by the MIT Press, Cambridge, Mass., and London, England.
Printed in the United States of America

10 9 8 7 6 5 4 3 2 1

For My Brother Spencer:

You're my north star, dude–
I remain in perpetual gratitude
to whatever forces of this universe that brought me you.
These poems could have never existed without our
talk-tunnels,
late-night postulations,
and of course, the soul-mating.

Stay gold, Ponyboy.

For Palestine, Tort, Refaat,
The Weelauhnee, & All the Bois:

¡Viva! ¡Viva!

CONTENTS

CHEST

The world is full of painful stories. Sometimes it seems as though there aren't any other kind and yet I found myself thinking how beautiful that glint of water was through the trees.

—Octavia E. Butler, *Parable of the Sower*

BLACK IDIOMS & EUPHEMISMS

Truth is, all Black people are poets—
we witchcraft like chemists
Can make a thing into another thing
with just a little imagination
I grew up so confused
about why so many things
that sounded good
were not actually good

Like
according to my childhood,
only a girl can be *fast*
in a bad way
and a boy fast
in the good one

Don't want a little *sugar in your tank*
And maybe that's why the world
has all this bite for me now
you know I—
I got that *sweet blood*

You didn't want to be *touched* or *special*
You'd better *stay on your shit* or you finna be
on that stuff when you grow up

Better to be a *latchkey kid* than to *smell like outside*
But me, the aunties say about me:
I can't hold water
I got loose lips
I skip home like *the street lights finna beat me*
smiled ripened with a secret

Even now, I wonder what will happen
the way I be carryin' on
telling the *outside* world
all about my *inside* business
you know,
the stuff I was told
better stay behind closed doors
I wonder if my childhood home—
the one that is boarded up
but still barking and baring teeth
in my memories—
will crumble with betrayal,
closed doors and all,
tumbling down like Jenga blocks
And someone thousands of miles away
knows the exact flavor of the *tea I'm spillin'*;
ears burnin' like hell

RISING ACTION LANDAY

i ask my therapist if a man
can be a daughter— she responds, “does he want to be?”

mommy-issues-ass-nigga-always
searching for a reason to call himself a hero

my whole life is an apology,
one I give myself in place of what you took from me

the irony isn’t lost on me:
sapphic awakening during *Edward Scissorhands*

the irony isn’t lost on me,
all of my favorite words begin with the prefix *trans*

every woman I have ever loved
has hesitated before placing her hand in mine

every good story needs a hero
every good hero undergoes a transformation

TRANSITORY

There is danger in the middle
I ignore the warning
of querying eyes
neither fish nor fowl
excess flesh
where only muscle
should protrude from chest bone
My body
a contested site
a meeting place
for White imaginaries
Brandon Teena's squelched laughter—
ground to ivory dust
somewhere in Nebraska[1]
a constant reminder
of what they might do to me
outside of a men's restroom
I chew my fears
into molars at night
trace them on lovers' backs
string together a personal history
from piecemeal memories
in case anyone asks
in case they write a book
in case someone wants to read
between the lines
in case I vanish

HOW TO SURVIVE A G*RLHOOD

Gay people weren't real in my house
I was an imaginary friend in my house
The first memory I have
Is of myself
Trying to wipe a memory away
Something torn and tender
Shrouded in fog
I wonder if I am both genders
Alien and mirage
Ambiance
And red flag
To be a girl is to constantly assess
What do I need to do *right now*,
To continue to be invited tomorrow?
I learned to blend into the background
Hid myself in closets
In fists
In another lost girl
Boy
Followed them like dyke Moses
Knowing damn well that
We could just be going
Further into the dark together
Into certain alienation
But sometimes it was worth it
Seeing other people from my planet
One time, I was invited into the boys club
But grown men showed up
Making themselves comfortable on my couch
Rough hands
Telling me
This is not permanent
What I am

Is definitely not something I want to be
That their goal
Is to fuck me into a sundress
But this is about much more than clothes
I can see past clothes—you feel me?
I would say my gender is Black
And that masculinity is just
How I relate to other beings
A state
An expression
A genre of human experience
When you ask me how I survived it, I say
I learned to send up a flare
I still naturally lilt my voice
Trauma bonds
And maybe some toxic ass nigga shit
But I'll be damned
If I'm going to be trapped in *your image of me*
Swallowed
On some slow, miserable death shit
If my younger self could see me now
They would ask
You chose yourself?
You're not scared to go to hell?
If my parents were still here,
Would I be this looking free?
Some girlhoods end in manhood
And we don't talk about those things
What isn't allowed under masculinity
What kept us from ourselves
And consumed with survival
I'm learning how to speak on it
Stand in it
Move in spaces
Embody the divine feminine

Honor the masculine
And see myself
One day I realized
I just don't have to give a fuck
I don't have to make my parents proud
I could just give myself permission
I already knew, I already felt
I know what my people look like
Whether you see us or not
And in the end
The conversation will always include me
Because Black women and queers
Will always be at the forefront of the struggle
Will always be at the forefront of the struggle
Will always be at the forefront of the struggle[2]

THE BODY (IN THEORY)

It's taken me over twenty years
to embrace this encasement,
manifest of all things
queer:
grotesque
  deviant
    handsome

        lovely

      still
      "Crooked Sternum is seeking one
      Surgical Steel Scalpel"

      like manic monarch screeching
      "off with their heads!"
          call it
      crown shyness
      I avoid touching
      entire regions of my body
      like they aren't there
      like I'm not there

      Don't see myself in some reflections
      only the kind ones
      with hands and tongues
      try to ignore
      something vampiric
      about my dysphoria—
      a shameful bloodlust
      Call to memory
      a time before
      the great betrayal

assigned fragile at birth
freakshow
f*g in two acts
fair-weather d*ke

finding something elsewhere

under the sky
under my skin
between my legs
between my lungs

I'd rather be bereft of such
unimportant flesh
and all the things we call ourselves in waking hours
savoring only the taut
and tender peel
only the remnants
only the bandage
only what is left behind

AGNOSTIC

I imagine you
peering down my throat
wishing the stars
into my gut
recounting
'If you look hard enough
a planetarium
a vast conservatory
all celestial knowings
and dark matter, too'
and though quite an honor
this ecology
to be the sky
take gracious form
a multiverse
housed in the small of me
I enjoy too much
being nothing
no aberration
fasten my lips

CHEST BINDER BLISS // TOP SURGERY BLUES[3]

I trace the indentations
where flesh and fabric
coalesce such that
I don't even recognize
My own reflection
And that feels good
My skin feels hot
and dense, a mountain of
me flattened to molehill and
I still want to be lessened

I feel along the scar line
meet for the first time
this body—forever mine
this new, foreign thing
is a dream awakened
but so damn scary
pain meds make me foggy
dysphoria shaped like
this new form, expands
although still tethered to

Backbone and sternum, marrowed and mired: *the bondage of this body*
Praise be the polyblend and good lighting, praise be the scalpel, the surgeon
The self-portraits because no one else knew how to conceal them in photos
Praise be the lovers who helped me pretend I was hollow from neck to navel
Sometimes, I still forget that they're gone, and that somehow, I'm still here
I sent a note to the anonymous recipient of my well-worn scrap of plastic
At first it said, please don't forget: a flat chest doesn't make you trans
And then I crossed that out and decided to write: this will crush you
bit by bit, a tiny suffocation every day—but it will feel like freedom

SEARCHING

(CL) atlanta > atlanta > community > missed connections

reply

It's true; I've been dying my whole life
to meet you, I take the longer routes home
boys suggest I stop fighting the current
fears keeping me up at night

This world is too massive
for this myopic urge, I write
you love letters and leave me a clue-
less mess to clean up if we find each other later

Recently, I've stopped wondering
if you really exist, you'll find me
wherever I am, I know this as true
love waits for no one

WHAT MEN ARE MADE OF

As a man of *new man* experience,
I've learned quickly
that I should aspire to be a *real man*,
you know, an OG,
a don, a honcho, a boss
the type of man who gets what he wants,
when he wants

I want to get the ingredients down,
don't want to get caught slippin',
so I look around
and take notes on the behavior of men—
jot down the essentials
The best recipe;
an ethnographic research study
of what makes a man
a man.
And I appreciate how helpful
they all are, teaching me things

Like yesterday,
I learned from watching a man,
who is old enough to be my granddaddy
call out to a girl
who is young enough to worship
Olivia Rodrigo and Normani,
how to get what I want, when I want

"You look nice today!"

She doesn't respond
and this is when Granddaddy teaches me
to speak *louder*,

just enough to spark a small flicker of fear

"You look nice today"

this time
barbed and bitter,
broken off like a glass bottle
held at the hip
but gripped with a grasp that says:
bitch, I will kill you

"Thank you!"

the girl manages to eke out
as she crosses the street

and it is then that I realize
men aren't made of masculinity,
testosterone,
oud tobacco aftershave
or steel-toe boots and bright ideas
like I'd always thought they were

Men are made of
"no, thank you"
bent into
"yes, please"
Men are very persuasive;
they can sell you a lemon
or your own life back to you
at twice the price
but you'd better respond nicely
To make a man:
you take the best parts of women,
add two fingers of whiskey,

then shake with fury
until the whole house is silent,
'till it ain't more *sweet shit*
knock it back
and keep your face
in placid repose
not no *weak shit*

"It still doesn't taste quite right"
I mumble
and a man
old enough to be my granddaddy
cuffs me at the ear,
leans in close,
the smell of oud tobacco aftershave
mixed with whiskey
pitches forward like a bad omen

"the fear,"

he hisses directly in my ear

"you forgot to add the fear"

PARABLE OF THE INNOCENT, OR BLACK TRANS-BOI ROADMAP

It's November, and babies are vanishing from the planet quicker than

[we]

would ever accept if they were anglo. And instead of organizing, or using our fists we

[must]

vote, according to the "in this house we believe" front yard sign liberals. The ones who

[swim]

in resort pools every summer, which have never cradled a Black body, but would swear

[through]

stark white veneers that they have Black friends and Brown ones and Yellow too and want

[the]

the world to be a safer place for this magnificent friend rainbow. Spewing white-hot

[swill]

like the promises made on a campaign trail. Leaving empty brown arms from Uvalde

[to]

Rafah—arms which now encircle only themselves until sleep comes. If this poem could

[reach]

anyone, I would want it to be a child who has not yet known suffering—a being barely beyond

[a]

twinkle in their father's eye. Unmarked by the pink and blue binary, or the red maga cap and

[pink]

pussy hat divide, or the billionaire versus the not-enough-food-to-feed-a-human-whose

-[nipple]-

needs-to-feed-another-human crisis. Yes, I hope this finds you still yet perfect, living in

[paradise]

HONEST BODIES CENTO

I conceive of my life
as a journey toward something:
anomalous intimacies,
the idioms of chemistry,
attempts to recover
what has been forgotten

We need to face the terrifying,
simple act of claiming pleasure;
that shattering or implosion of self,
the deviancy assigned to evolution

Imagine our predicament
if we coexisted,
intertwined with new high-pink flesh,
buoyantly dressed,
before the summer solstice

Sweat bees and mud daubers,
call them freedom fighters,
—brow puckered and sucking teeth—
find fault, cling,
reject the path we have cleared,
its angular turns ruptured
in Washington's sweltering heat

And still,
I view them with hope
and not despair
Everybody knows somebody
readying up for honesty,
and moments of transcendence
They have simply been taught
not to speak the truth of their bodies

LINGUICISM

despite the violent summer heat
i reveled in the shared warmth of our palms,
bound together by tenuous finger lacings
we struggled for discussion
took gaudy gulps of tepid water from your bottle
both of us keenly aware
that the season's end was near
our latent togetherness was doomed
i snuck a glance at you
spied the smudge of raspberry jam on your chin
rubbed it away tenderly with my free thumb
you pursed your lips
with tacit resentment
toward my small, loving act
the sun perched hauntingly
shone boastful rays on your fast-rosing cheeks
i prayed that the words, coiled tightly in my chest,
would slip outward and stir you
perhaps you would reward me with a sweaty, august grin
but before i could form the syllables
a final, wistful incantation
i felt coolness meet the dampened belly of my grasp—
your hand no longer in mine

LEMONS

In truth,
I am *hopeless* at being hopeless about love
I look for love in its most impossible hiding places
Like: my living room couch
inside a jar of Nutella
inside a dark movie theater
inside a dark memory

I act like love is just playing hard to get with me
I act like I am not hard to love
I act like love hasn't been hard on me;
like I haven't spent every year
as far back as I can remember
seeking a love that would make me feel lovable

I chase it into the wind like scattered seeds,
hoping to see it sprouting come springtime,
but knowing this Carolina clay doesn't soften
for most blossoms

I hunker down–black-thumbed–tongue poking out,
looking for love in a pocket-sized computer,
saving my greatest poems for the inbox of somebody's daughter,
sulking and sullen when I am left on *seen*
I was never very good at partner poetry,
I have to remind myself to leave room
for someone else's stanzas;
I've always balked
at meeting someone else's standards,
but I'm sure for the right one
I could rise to the occasion

I think the times are telling me to give up on love
As a species,
we might be coming to a close
sooner than we'd predicted

I wonder if my "one" is close by,
somewhere, closed off,
telling herself I am not looking for her either,
having been sold lemons
and fools gold
an untold number of times in my absence

I'm sure she is the pessimist to my optimist,
and that's what makes us perfect for one another,
and potentially doomed never to meet each other
Without even knowing her,
I know we are each strong enough to live without the other,
a truth designed to devastate us both.

I tell everyone in my life I've given up–
thrown in the towel,
this fruitless search for an elusive love
feels like a losing battle
and I am *exhausted*

But in truth, I am hopeless
at being hopeless about love
So, even as I delete the apps,
stop looking around every bar
and coffee shop
with an eager eye–
convince myself that my wanting her
is a projection
of something not yet healed in me,

quietly, there is a small flame
that continues to flicker in my chest
Yes,
I have stood up,
walked deliberately toward the threshold of my world
and gently,
pushed the front door shut.
But, just before I turn to walk away,
I make a last-minute decision
to leave it unlocked
You know,
just in case

RIBS

It is sheer good fortune to miss somebody long before they leave you.

—Toni Morrison, *Sula*

+1 (310)
Torrance, CA
December 31, 2024 at 4:07 AM
0:00
–0:37
Transcription
"Hey Kelsey I'm
leaving
but are you falling
let me know
OK..."

Favorites

Recents

Contacts

Keypad

21
Voicemail

REVISIONIST HISTORY

I haven't even begun to grieve you
before the trauma starts taking bites
the truth, falling into question
and too, my heart a landmine
tearing limbs, telling lies
for all that you were
an open palm
a closed fist
fingers
nails

THIRSTY

It's a sleight of hand, I realize exactly too late
you play a woodwind,
and instead of a cobra dance,
yellow canaries beak their way
out through my earholes,
flapping around your head, so miserably in love
we are in front of my childhood home
and I am ashamed
of how boring it is in comparison
to your silken shirt
garish, wildeyed expression
I want to live with you I think
I want to go to every place with you
And while you always say nothing,
I am certain that this is shared between us
Look at my canaries, and how they halo your perfect,
perfect head

But you are looking past them,
your eyes tracing my lips hungrily
And wordlessly, your hand lifts from your side
You're doing it wrong, I don't protest
when your fingers grasp the small, shimmering ribbon,
a yardlong bean,
poking out of the corner of my mouth;
you must have planted it in me some night
and in one swift tug, we are both stunned
when an impossibly
too-many things come heaping out:
The spoons that you hid under the couch
to avoid your mother's rage
tied to the crabs your uncle bought you
well, really just the one–

you know, the juicy one, that ate the other one
ate its middle clean out
when you forgot to feed them
tied to the chairs
we flirted circles around
on the day we met,
tied to the books I read to impress you
tied to the books I lied and said I read
to impress you,
tied to my ribcage, so suddenly,
I fall over
broken and gelatinous,
looking up to find you
cooing over my brow,
the guilt pooling at your eye-corners
falling only the once,
directly into my open mouth
down my throat, to join all of the other things
that had become untethered,

"you wont leave me here, will you?" I manage
as you disassemble the woodwind,
kicking astray the the rubble
the canaries, now frantic,
hopping about at your feet
still so ready to fly
so ready to *dance for you*

In the distance, I see a neighbor dog
pittering across lawns,
lapping at a gutter drain
Damn, that looks so good,
I think to myself;
the animal of me
aware for the first time in weeks

of my basic survival needs
I am so horrendously thirsty

Then, there is the sun,
seeming to drop from the sky in an instant,
and you are also gone
The canaries are pecking at my cheeks,
tangling in my hair
hoping to find their way back
The neighbor dog turns toward me,
seems to contemplate
whether I am food,
fun,
trash,
or threat,
and just before he turns his head away,
the light brown brindle of his coat
becomes livened under the streetlight

Not the neighbor dog, I slowly remember
he had died a few years back
Who would rebound all of me
that had become unspooled,
I wonder–
the canaries finally quieted
And then, I am quieted
Asleep like that, confetti all over a driveway
And then I am dreaming of you again:
your perfect, *perfect* head,
You, and that sweet little dog, I imagine
No, not *dog*
Not dog, *coyote*
Good puppy,
sharp puppy

THE IDEA OF SOMEONE KWANSABA[4]

Who were you when you kissed me?
Loved me up so good I forgot
myself, and lost all of my reserve
I think that you're my best thought
An urban mirage of my own making
Even when I see you, I don't
I see who I want to see

LIGHT RAIL

–After Jessica Abughattas

The heart isn't interested in change
The heart wishes to return to the site of love
over and over,
finding everything in its proper place

The heart wants to know who the fuck
moved all of its things around
The heart remembers with precision
where these things belong
The heart will get to the bottom of this

The heart isn't interested in ego death,
or any kind of death, really
The heart insists on a measure of certainty—
permanence
The heart is aghast
to learn that death is the next best thing

When the heart finds itself
in conversation with another heart,
it talks too much
too quickly
telling half-truths because
who doesn't love a little razzle-dazzle

When the heart is sad
it watches sad movies
in order to make itself more sad
and strangely, this makes the heart less sad
the heart is a little kinky like that

The heart has good intentions,
it's the execution that falters
The heart is an aries with an aquarius moon
so it loves a pinch of chaos and
a dash of mystery

The heart is a real sweetie pie, a honey boy
Sure, the heart is a bit self-involved but
the heart has been in therapy for the past five years
and is working on it

It's just *time*, really
The heart is always racing time
and how time always brings change
The heart is so sensitive about that
The heart is so easily lost
easily turned around
and that is why the heart doesn't take well
to re-arrangement

The heart keeps everything in its place
in order to stay on schedule
Stay oriented
Stay on the fastest, most direct route
The heart isn't interested in life as a highway,
the heart prefers a train track, *a light rail*
The heart needs to know where it's headed
Needs to be able to find its way back

MASCULINITY & FEMININITY[5]

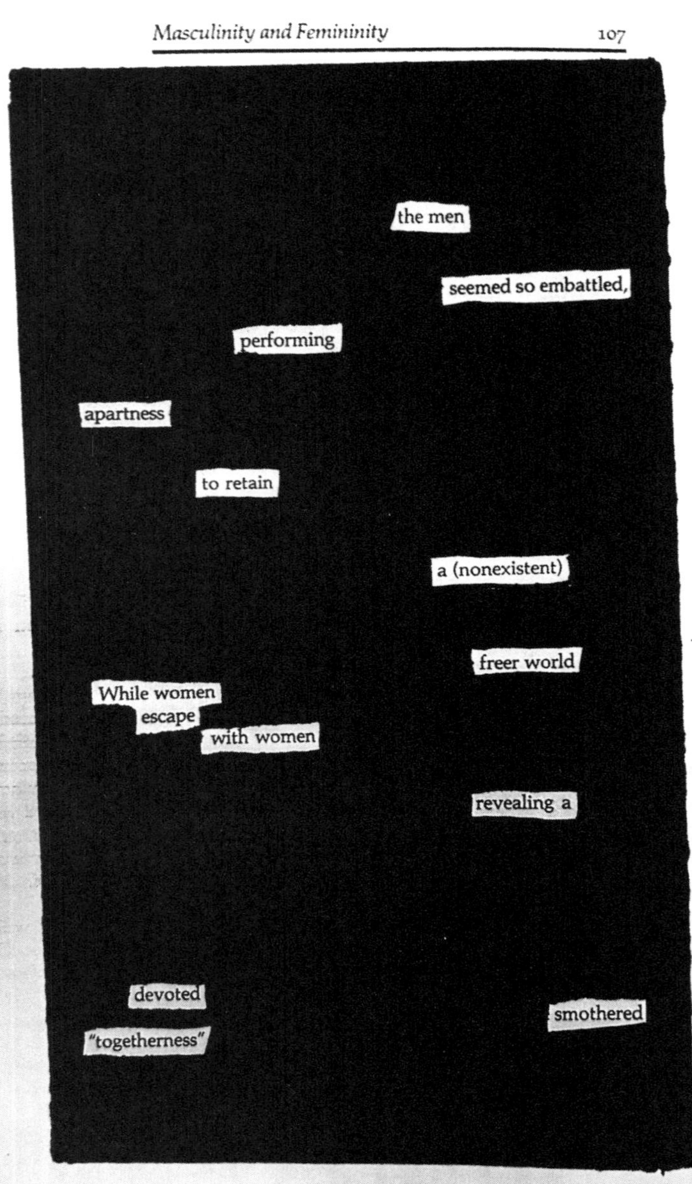

A.B. PERSONA POEM—A GOLDEN SHOVEL

—After Patricia Smith's Always in the Head

I like sharing this earth with you.
I like how, on a granular level, we are just
two occurrences, made of the same things as milkshakes and molten lava. You take
the best pictures of me. No, I don't look particularly pretty, but I'm firmly in
the moment with you. I wonder about the day in which the
archive will spill my secrets. Will some young writer, or thinker, or lover see the word
madly written across all of my journals and just as easily unearth you?
I wonder what I can leave behind that could make someone know,
or not know all of the ways in which I spiraled, flitting about
your apartment like a bat—blood-shot and frantic—looking for somebody
just like you. Somebody who could make this all worth it, the living and the dying.

~~BOY~~ BOI

i like a boi
how this boi laughs in boi-ish ways
like me
but not like me
we touch like bois
a little rough
together, make a boihood
no context nor precedent for how my
hands find boi
body
trembles under
boi fingers
how they knead and need
their
lightning strikes red hot how and where
i touch their boihood
their hands on my designer
boi chest
i know that they can feel
my boi heart knocking
against spare ribs
wonder if it makes me less
of a real boi
how much of my being boi
was bolstered by being
uninterrupted by another boi
how much of becoming a boi
means rejecting other bois
i take in panicked boi breaths
feel like boi meets world
when i stare into boi eyes
get tripped up
start to wonder

if this is what they meant
by bois will be bois

PEPPER JACK

i belong to myself these days
hasn't always been that way a stranger i
used to call mom still four hot embers in my mind's eye
still a cuss and a key-turn and fast footsteps
up the stairs
you don't belong to you photographs charred
at the corners jeer
if i look too closely back at me
or them or her
i still wrestle with my body so used to playing tug-of-war
over myself that even the half left limp and
dangling still feels
like someone is trying to wring me out
like a water-logged rag
i marvel at my scars my tattoos with a hint of indignation
like the biggest fuck you i could give was to draw
on the walls rip up the carpet threaten to raze and break

these good bones down to the studs and build back

something i like better

i guard myself too closely at times throw

molotov cocktails at passersby

who look in my direction i try to explain

in therapy

that my home training was more boot camp than

debutant i don't know the right forks

or words to use to make people

understand that i do want them close but i

still need to sit facing the exit

i think i will spend the rest of my life sneaking

into the kitchen after dark eating handfuls

of shredded cheese

like it's my birthright no forks necessary

i forgive those four hot embers for all of my

burns

that stranger i used to call mom

don't blame her for how much she wanted

me to belong to her

i am so damn good i know that much i am

someone

you might want a piece of i am still

learning how to share

ELEGY FOR A *BLACK* BUTCH BOI

we the never
dear but departed
gathered then scattered
in less than 30 dyke bars
across the country
and homegirls' houses
plus that one guy's
who tried to fuck
but moved on
when he realized
we wasn't with it

we just here for
last respects
better known as
last month's rent
and deposit
on the love nest
we rushed into

we indulgent
like soul food
maybe not the healthiest
but shit
paying two rents was
unhinged behavior
and she had that good shit
worth dying under
every night

we neither coquettish
nor fetish
served in every selfie

i was never finna smile
in that photo
i don't care that you wanted
me to pull up my pants
or wear a dress
like the other bridesmaids
bury me casket fresh
in j's on a friday

we the glue of this family
though you would never admit it
what else is keepin y'all together

like the gossip do
tryna guess if she my roommate
where our boyfriends at
if she play basketball too
with the low fade
but granny still
give her a little lemonade
when she come around
'cause she a pretty little thing
'not like that bulldagger'
granny say
that ol' manly girl
from around the way

we the lost causes
they stopped using that line
'you might like dick if you tried it'
a long time ago
slang that thang
if we pulled up with a back-pack
and that's on period
if you know you know

funny thing is–
we bisexual
but we gon die a goldstar
rather than
let a nigga talk to us like
we not that nigga forreal

we the
never got a childhood
because our mamas
didn't want us having sleepovers
with girls or boys
we the never got a pap smear

        or a mammogram
        because we couldn't afford the shit
        and even if we could
        afford the shit
        we the please don't touch me
                                this body is my armor

we built ford-tough
we not bitch-made

we dead at the tender age
of 38
we still some babies
on our death day
we the tacit tether
we the roots
we like a coda to this hard Black life
we the original sin
we holy
reimagined at the repast

we back to being good christian girls
we just some raisins in the sun

TWINKLE MAN

Nhat begins each sentence by saying
"I think my favorite thing about being Haitian is"
And then he changes the end of his sentence every time

First, his favorite is the fierceness of the fight,
and too, the gentle unwavering spirit

Nhat yells when he talks;
Makes sure you know when he's coming
Makes sure you know where his mouth is from

Nhat says his favorite thing about being a Haitian,
is that they don't care what anybody thinks:
That they are a people who can 'smile in the face of a sneer'

I've never seen Nhat take a single step
Rather, he glides across every room
The kompa in his stride keeping his hips loose

I've never seen a smile like his on a man before
Never known a man who would let his smile wear his entire body
He is beautiful, in the way a pearl necklace is
And honestly, I don't know if he knows his own glimmer

I spend my Friday evenings in Nhat's living room,
at least, that's what it feels like to me because isn't this the room
in which I do my best living
He doesn't know how much of my life he has gifted back to me
Doesn't know I am *only* fearless as a space explorer

Nhat says Haitian food is the best in the world
and as the griot melts on my tongue I don't dare deny that

I might not be a zo, but I know we kin
because we both prefer our pigs beheaded and fried

Nhat turns a small room in Kennesaw into a revolution
But I grimace when Nhat calls himself 'Nathaniel'
instead of *Nhataniel*,
Says his name is spelled funny
like this America who sits so violently between us
isn't the joke

Nhat's eyes twinkle like sparklers at a wedding
I see both the fierce and the gentle in his lineage
I haven't known him since a youth,
but I know it was always the *twinkle* that gave him away

He explains that he is only *'blond'* when he is unsure of himself
Says within or outside of Ayiti, he is always *'of the home'*,
—wears his sense of wonder like a badge of honor, right next to his flag

I know his eyes are trained south,
keeping the idea of his home as elsewhere

But I hope he knows as brothers of the diaspora
we will always find homes
in one another

I hope he knows
he has helped me to make a home out of myself

In his presence,
I feel like I am the man I always dreamt myself to be
I hope he knows
MWEN KA APRANN RENMEN'L NAN LANG MANMAN LI

WATER NOMADS

In sex, I never let myself be flower
never let myself be a thing of beauty
never bloom beneath the dancing shadows of the cityscape
reflected through the dark

I'd rather not be saught,
displaced,
taken home as garnish

I'd rather be thorn–
knife
body a fortress
rather stay rooted
rather be stick than stuck
rather count the petals of my lovers one by one,
deciding whether or not love is in the room with us

Rather be buck and thrust than grip and gasp
Rather be spectator than spectacle
Rather be fern;
nimble and spindle
or forest:
deep and dark and wild,
a danger for those looking for a hunting ground,
those seeking to mount me as trophy

In sex, I keep score
Tally-marks from finger nails
I carry a lover to where the waves break
Make my body a shelter
from the wake's violent crashing
Aching number's the morning,
but we do not hold one another's wounds for ransom

We get busy again like we
do this to keep ourselves afloat
and I–
the *not-flower* that I am,
fashion myself into lily pad
to cradle a lover;
keep their blossom safely perched,
bloomed wide open
while I maintain a barrier
between what I think could kill me,
and what I think might heal me

SONNET FOR THE INDECISIVE

trans math is realizing at thirty
that you like boys as much as you are one
meaning a lot, and not really at all
meaning maybe I never believed in

this ungodly mess of prefab bodies
can you truly call it a transition
when you exist as both—also neither
maybe the future is genderfucked, not

female like we'd hoped that it would be and
maybe since the rules are made up I can
retire that little part of me that
still balks when someone calls me beautiful

still wonders if I'm going through a phase
as if that makes me any less human

LUNGS

Something has to be done about the way in which this world is set up.

—June Jordan, *Some of Us Did Not Die: Selected Essays*

WHAT DIDN'T HAPPEN WHEN WE KISSED

We missed. Stuttering the air between us with the faintest brush of lips and cheek before parting sheepishly, surmising that this false start was a signifier—a clear indication that we had been mistaken | We felt nothing, our kiss lacking that mien of heady gusto we had been fighting, my hands then timid and uncertain, finding the skin at your collar prickled like roughly sawn lumber. Too, while we hovered loosely in the orbits of one another, I found you devoid of your signature vanillic musk | We pecked politely. Hyper-aware of onlookers, both of us historically modest in temperament, our meeting of mouths was brief, platonic, and perfunctory. Afterward, we fist-bumped and walked in opposite directions | We lacked synchronicity. We flailed. Our teeth knocked as we struggled for a rhythm. The twin storms of us raged in opposing spirals, leaving no discernable pathway toward connection | We recoiled, dismayed to find ourselves mutually repulsed by the taste. Expecting Maraschino cherries with a hint of southern comfort, we were greeted with the pinch of something that had long-soured | We knew we would be unaffected by it as soon as it began, so unremarkable as it was, we knew we would never even remember this kiss; this merging of something dissimilar to heartbeats. This tepid attempt at meaning-making, breathing life into a chance, though lukewarm, encounter | We were rushed because of your approaching bus | We were distracted, both preoccupied with the coming day and its demands | We were hungry, our stomachs growling in syncopation | And exhausted, unable to spare a single second more for the fleeting flutter of this feeling | And in the days after, the kiss is so far from our minds. It does not float overhead, haunting us at the grocery store, growing particularly pronounced as we cradled a handful of ripened plums | It certainly does not begin to blare at the full volume as we drive past the street corner where the kiss took place: that ever-growing lifetime ago | It didn't captivate, excite, or terrify us, both the thought of doing it, and never doing it again. To the contrary, it is forgotten, a fever dream, a far-off figment of stillness, a solitary act of measured investigation. When we kissed, I did not fall in love with you. Nor did you with me. I did not come to crave you like water, and you did not find yourself, for years on end, wishing to find yourself ducked under the canopy of me again, seeking that strange simultaneity of danger and safety. We both hated that kiss and all the things it never meant to us. For this, I am grateful.

HOW TWO DEPRESSIVES MANAGE COEXISTENCE

we take turns
being tethered
one, spirited away
the other making tea

we watch one another
wilt
wither
crack a chapped lipped grin
every now and again
easily mistaken for a grimace
by someone who has never cried
because sunlight poured in

sometimes
we speak in hushed tones
whisper into the other's neck
sometimes we howl
from somewhere
deep and hollow
but unabiding

'it won't always ache like this
it won't always ache like this'

perch two fingertips lightly
just below the jaw
oh good,
one might think

you're still with me, you're still here

some days
we push the furniture against the walls
play Chaka Khan and shimmy at one other
cook that pasta from last winter
ignore the strange texture
look almost healthy
hold one another
and feel new bones

some days we shuffle coldly
past one another
cut eyes and kiss teeth
and speak with venom
it's your fault I'm like this,
we think and don't mean

but then, the sun retreats
and we emerge like night bugs
scurry around one another in small circles
touch hands,
mouths,
cling to the heat of one another's bodies,
forget for just a short while
that we are two separate beings
fighting the night

we sweat and weep
and try to make sense of how fortunate we are
to have found one another
in all of this unluck

one gathers the other up in their arms
one mumbles something about needing to do the dishes
one drifts slowly into slumber
one stays painfully awake,

tasked with surviving the quiet
alone, again

we do puzzles, we read,
we talk about people we knew when we were young,
we eat,
we don't eat,
we journal, we sleep
we sleep,
we sleep,
we look out the window,
we try to remember who we were before this,
we kiss each other's temples, and then

some days we open the front door,
feeling like babies in tuxedos
or martians cosplaying millennials
out of our pajamas, in real clothes
ready to brave the grocery store

you go ahead,
one says, suddenly unsure
as they catch a glimpse of the world
for what feels like the first time in years
I think I'll stay here

after a pause, the other
steps back from the doorway
turns and offers a solemn nod,
reaches out
takes the other's hands
and then, in a familiar
convivial tone, responds
before I go, would you like some tea?

NIGHT BALM QUATERN

the boy in me needs to be held
needs ear pressed to chest—nose to neck
needs breath dancing across forehead
creamsicle sky slipping from sight

your fingers curl in my hair when
the boy in me needs to be held
you tend to him like broken skin
apply pressure where he purples

i struggle to still in the night
a guineafowl caught in a snare
the boy in me needs to be held
a chickpea at your palm's center

morning breaks like the man of me
you smile into my stubble
reminding me not to fear that
the boy in me needs to be held

we gleamed that prom night, like lit lightning bugs, flossy something sincere; our mamas gruffed up and flummoxed about wingtip shoes, and us carrying on with girls like they were boys. no small joys, despite the knowledge that we were headed to disparate camps which would teach us how to better be—we danced that night, you and me, like we had the right and nerve to insist upon one last solstice of far flung freedoms. all of us clambering for a little something sweet, but feigning sour in the moonlight—something dour in the limelight. we liked to cosplay like we some eastside niggas, all puffed up and out, but we still wet behind the ears so i know you finna blush when you read the poems i wrote about you. i never forgot the summer you told me you'd take me out to the country and fry me up some field snakes, or the way he never knew he wasn't blood but kinfolk just the same. how could i have foreseen the way our fireside chats would take us coast to coast, lyin' to ourselves in every city, thinking we could shake these listless, bogged down, half-baked, pre-stretched personas? i'm your biggest fan but you treat me like your biggest opp. at least i ain't no damn cop, and you left the marine corps with nothing but a few scratches. i thank god or whoever's out there for my baby boys, and the way i know how to code switch but fight the instinct every chance i get. maybe this fancy paper won't make me a real nigga but i can use it to keep us safe, you and me. i love you like how daddies supposed to love their first-born sons and i don't like to look at that too close. i love me like how mamas supposed to hate their daughters and i can't look away. i wouldn't change how it happened for anything though. i'm just saying.

YOU CAN SWIM UNDERWATER, JUST DON'T BREATHE IN

fluidity has come to encompass
my mainstay sadness
my only optimism
you, like me, are sea

whether spraying or sucking
sinking, even in shallow streams
treading tirelessly
or floating with resignation

hot springs comprised of teardrops
the summertime pitcher of sweet tea
the ease with which
you sweat me out

swallowing lake norman
hot chocolate before bed
spittle well spent on heated exchanges
bleeding out the last of it

i smear the remnants of swamp water
on the dew-kissed grass
piss all over your good name
start swimming

BLACK TRANS MAN KILLED BY POLICE IN FLORIDA[6]

TONY MCDADE WAS

trans was killed was

promising the day before.

The man who died

the complex McDade was unarmed did not resist However, Police had a gun and

shot never any
warning before shooting.

just

gunshots

the
life

of McDade

was taken,
made public
The officer who shot McDade is on paid
administrative leave

Still, the community is
gathering where he was shot with posters reading
"Justice for Tony."

GRIEF KWANSABA

On the day the word still spun
I tried to recall the deep quiet
that we could have lived in forever
I loved sharing this life with you
Now, I always burn the brown rice
I scamper from a tepid shower, alone,
to our bed, empty of warm bodies

STORIES WE TELL OURSELVES

Sometimes, I look at you, and you are a heartbreak.
And still, I tell myself at least twice a year that I am not
in love with you. *And still*, every day besides those two,
I am haunted by the way you look in a crowd.
How your face is impossibly distinct amidst a sea,
how immediately I find your eyes, and how, before
I can tell it not to, *my* face is already splitting open.
And of course, you are smiling too, because how
could you not smile when someone looks at you
the way that I do? And then, the time it takes for us to
cross the sea turns into days, and then weeks,
and then you are in my arms and we are rocking like
old friends. Ones who know we should have
gotten married when we were young and lacking
foresight. And when we are done rocking,
you slip away, and it is my heart that realizes before
my arms. And then it is the cheek that was pressed against
yours. My brain finally catches on when I register
that your silhouette is moving toward the horizon.
And still, nothing seems to make me not be in love with you.
And still, I keep telling myself that I am not.
And still, I am not listening.

THE REVOLUTION MIGHT NOT BE TELEVISED

. . . but *shit*
it might be on signal
you might catch it on vanish mode
on the bat-phone
all my kinfolk got two names
two phones
all my niggas got two jobs
all my boifriends got two scars
from where their shame was cut free
all my friends are *too* tired to hangout these days
all my nightmares got fangs on 'em these days
don't have to go to the movies to catch a blood-bath
the revolution won't be on *tik tok*
'cuz they finna cancel that shit
too bad we only got *two* parties in this country,
and neither of them are lit
all my aunties say "it takes *two* to tango"
but i got two left feet,
so i'm hangin' up my dancin' boots
last time i fell in love with a real
down-to-mars-girl
i got caught *two-timing*
and them *two* new tires
were expensive as fuck
all my slimes need root canals
need the change
that was supposed to come in 2020
when we all took to the streets
and *risked our lives* in an attempt to stop *risking our lives*
all my day-ones don't give a fuck
they'll pull up on you if i text them "ski mask"
make you *two-step* with a two-piece

all my poems are about Palestine now
even if i don't say it outright
my anger, my heartbreak—
the gall of this fucked up place
to keep changing the rules
keep making little angels
and then turning them into ancestors
before their sweet-sixteens
all my shorties got *two-plus* baby daddies
'cuz we pro-hoe on this side
and even if the revolution won't be televised
it might be live-streamed
once they drink a little too much tequila
and start talkin' that talk for real
all my babies will be free someday
i know it
well, maybe not my babies,
but my babies' babies

if the world even lasts that long
if we even have enough drinkable water
and the polar bears aren't gone
all my people are going with me
don't really know where we're going,
or how we're going to know
if we made it,
we're just going,
on some *parable of the sower* type shit.
and maybe,
maybe we won't even make it.
shit—
maybe we'll all just die some revolutionaries

HOW TWO DEPRESSIVES MANAGE COEXISTENCE PT. II

we take turns
feeding one another
with food we can't afford
we break up
and stay together

we attend one another's funerals
amazed each time
that the other is still alive
we thrive
for a flurry of fleeting moments
we shimmer and glimmer like trophies
too heavy to carry home
but beautiful to behold

we dance in the rays
of one another's moonbeams
and too, become convinced
that we are dark matter
something so unknowable
to anyone but ourselves
and one another

we pick the skin
from one another's folding limbs
we hold the heat from forgotten words
deep in our throats
and when we breathe outward
we beg spirit for new homes
suddenly aware
that we are walking wildfires

and though sometimes we are kind
we are always kindling
we touch sternums
turn backs
shout, in jubilation
seethe, in quiet panic

we drum full belly anthems for silly dances
we find fairy-tale reasons to avert our eyes
and we cry
we cry and we cry
and we sleep
and sleep for too many hours

until one of us
takes the other's hand
pulls it into the cool
air of night
unafraid of the dirge,
and the dirt-devil-speckled earth
that one goes first
turns to face the other but
cannot find the words
and so
the other takes a stab
at unsatisfying the silence
points to nowhere in particular
and says, quietly
yes, i get it
but both is better, i believe

REQUIEM FOR A GONE GIRL

I've kissed at least one dead girl that I know of. I look back and realize she was maybe only barely alive when we kissed. Tawny girl, whose limbs I heard crumpled inward towards the end. The one-time teen dream queen who introduced the Gretchen's to x pills and tongue-tying cherry stems. I thought she didn't like me at first, which made me work harder to impress her. Then, I acted like I didn't like her at all, and that was the golden ticket. Back then, I didn't realize how my Blackness towered statuesque between me and the White kids. One told me his dad knew exactly where my family lived, in our seemingly infinite grid of houses, all more or less the same. Still, he knew exactly. Anyway, me and the then-alive girl kissed in her bathroom. And when she didn't text me back that night, I felt like a sad dog, the memory of the kiss like a milk bone that had toppled behind the toilet. Back then, kisses felt like gold stars, or the Jolly Ranchers my 5th-grade teacher would tuck into my jacket pocket. For being *so smart*, she'd said, the candy slightly melted by the warmth of her folded palm. I never knew whether "*for a Black girl*" was implied. Anyway, back to the other girl, the *only girl*, really—the one who died. I remember her kisses were soft staccato, the kind a mother puts on a crying toddler's forehead. And I'm sure that I responded, wound up as I was, with wet eager smooches. I never saw her again after that day. She died before twenty-five. But I got the sense, I wouldn't have seen her again, even if she'd survived that suburban listlessness. I wasn't her type. Fumbling-bumbling teenaged juggernaut, tongue-tied and sweet like a cherry. Too clean. Too pristine. Too alive.

ELSEWISE

The sun sets
under the horizon.
Well-rested
from being down all day,
I unmake the bed,
unbrew some coffee,
and unthink about you.

My thoughts lag—
I unstretch,
feeling every muscle tighten.
In the shower,
I make the water as cold
as I can tolerate
before freezing my skin.
My heart, *so light,*
so together.
I reread every text
you unsent.

Hadn't I been
unreasonable?
Is this love truly
unending?
For the remainder
of the evening,
I become increasingly
unsure
of how I feel.

I am utterly
underwhelmed
by the thought of you,
unhappy with someone else.

SELF-PORTRAIT AS PI

we three   not-girls   not-boys

all grit   all iris   too loud   in our mothers'

living rooms

too ugly for a prom date   ripened   through

pubescent fantasy

ready   to come alive   nobody to come alive

with

we three   like porcelain figurines   collecting dust

on our mothers' dresser-tops   sneaking phone calls

          in our closets

secret kisses   at an all-girls sleepover   while

boy-brained

trapped in a girl's body   we like hiccups   in our

mothers' throats

chipping away   at a jack-and-jill destiny   we all

fresh stink

and still baby in the face   but we fast-fast

just not on the racing track

hurtling ourselves beyond the grasp of our

neighborhoods

hanging out with girls with names like goddess and

serenity

meanwhile they anything but

we three vagabonding trying to fill a void

thorns in our mothers' sides shame in our

mothers' hearts

we grow crooked out suburban soil all the

things we coulda been

we chose hairy and hard-headed we three could be

so pretty

if we would learn to mind our elders

keep our legs closed

we coulda been a miracle—we three

or a bullet train or a ceo in our own right

instead, we pencil shavings in the wind

bruised peaches

not the girls   our mothers prayed for

        we slick in the mouth

hot in the pants   we might never amount   to

anything

just here   letting all the good air   out the house

taking up space   doing everything   we not supposed to

come to find out   it's all we can do   cuttin' up like this

grinning wild   like hyenas   too wild even

        for our ancestors' dreams

        but quietly   we wonder if we finna be   bigger

than ourselves   someday

a part of something   revolutionary   we three

like fruit flies

circling an altar   hungry for an offering   or like

horseflies

thrashing into elbows   refusing to still our bodies

and be a mirror on the wall   we rather be nasty like a water bug

make them people   crawl out their skin   fall away

from girlhood

like we did it before   like we back from somewhere

like we some ghosts   who never believed in

ghosts

never believed the preacher   or our mothers

or the daddies

just that we   belong to one another   like we

three could make

a different type of world   like we goin' somewhere for real

tracing fingers over palms   in bathroom stalls

making maps for

someone else to follow

until then,   we resolute   stay not-girls

not-boys   stay black   and die

the only thing   we three   are good for

HEART

When you reach out and touch other human beings, it doesn't matter whether you call it therapy or teaching or poetry.

—Audre Lorde, *Conversations with Audre Lorde*

because you come up in my house, pouring yourself big cups of the juice I buy from the farmer's market, knowing damn well how much it costs, and I'm steady smiling—grateful you still have a mouth with which to drink. To be real, I'm just honored to witness you. We dance in my kitchen, drunk, making 3 am egg sandwiches while listening to Glorilla, and you wait until I've already called your Uber before you begin to cry. In an instant, my arms are around your neck and we are so quiet. You whisper "*my nigga, they were so young*" and I nod against your melted cheek, and when you get up to leave, I am terrified of how my heart follows. We call each other *twin* and *my g*, and I try to tamp down the masculinity hulking between us. But it's always been so fun with you: pretending we are big and bad together, scattering across the suburbs as two misfits, boys with Kool-Aid smiles and quick tempers. Now, we stand in this kitchen as self-made mercurial men, holding one another, weeping for all of the people who no longer have mouths with which to drink.

I love you, I love you, I love you twin

is an incantation over your head to keep you safe, and here, even when you are hurting. Even when you go to that far-off place inside of yourself where I can't protect you. I know I love you because I am hurting too. Because I feel gorgeous under your watchful eye. Because we have never quite known what to say to one another, but our shared quiet is a soak in Epsom salt and chamomile. I know I love you when I crawl into bed, open our text thread, and watch the small blinking circle of you as it traces the web of streets between us. I shut my eyes only when I'm certain that you've made it home.

IF I MUST LIVE

—After Refaat Alareer

no one will ever be able to convince me that Refaat needed to die— *no one.*
but if i must live my life in a world absent his, i won't shut up about it. no, i won't march toward nightfall
keening into the void. i'll insert a little genocide into your light-hearted brunch conversation. i will knuck
if you buck; i will make you say loudly and with your chest that you don't give a fuck about the dead babies
so long as yours stays plump and rosy-cheeked. i try to grant Refaat's wishes and bed my words
into hope. but my poems come out with aimed
precision brandished like weapons. perhaps
this was the plan all along: to make
us monsters too. angry enough to
lose our humanity, blast holes into
people like we ain't just want to live
and hold our babies up
toward the morning sky.

GLORY DAYS

Before I was a baby, I was a beautiful idea.
The salvation of a Jersey girl whose limbs hung
grotesquely, draped in berry-blue defiance, whipped
in all white till her dress frayed and fell cherry-stained
on the long walk home. A Brooklyn boy's respectable
manifest destiny as he sprouted upwards, toward the
heavens, from a roach-infested tinsel tower varnished
in my grandfather's secrets. I was part and parcel,
the means of production. I could make a dream
so American it'd twinkle like onyx,
buffed and chiseled into a vanity. So reflective,
they could almost see themselves in me.
& then I was ugly.

One does not become ugly overnight, there is a context
for such monsterfication; it takes a learned imperfection.
Cracked teeth in a mouth that insists upon staying open
and so much self you spill out of yourself. You become
the answer to questions no one ever planned on asking like:
How are you yo daddy's son when you'supposed to be
a daughter? Couldn't you color yourself lighter in every hue?
Couldn't you walk lighter than a feather,
instead of this hulking beast, a blight, refusing
to be the beautiful through-thread of this story?
And who the fuck do you *think you are*
being this ugly and unabashed?

And then I was hands and snap and sparkle
puppeteering in the morning light.
And then I was boy, embodied
and benevolent. And then I was handsome, hanging
on your every word. And then I was gravel voice
and gray-evening-haloed in tobacco
& then I was beautiful again.

I couldn't keep pretending I wasn't. Lips berried
with vulgar smarts. A fifth of whiskey easy
on the way down. A baby-eyed big talker.
One does not become beautiful overnight.
There is a ceremony in this release.
There is grief in the cutting away of flesh.
In the leap from the jetty. It is an ugly feeling, truly,
to touch your own beauty for the first time and realize
how many years you denied yourself to yourself.
How you foraged and flailed and reached for the things
furthest from your own face,
catching fistfuls of nothing but the quiet.
How you believed in a god
not strong enough to see themselves in you.

How you let them make you into a monster,
or a fantasy, or salvation
like you weren't an offering.
Like you weren't conjured from the people
in every corner of the planet.
Like you might spend your whole life
apologizing for the things they could not hold,
for all of the ways in which you are wayward.

But mostly, for making them into lies–*liars.*
How you never saw what they saw when they saw you.
How you never defined the sun by the way it looks
dipping below the horizon, never allowed the thunderclap
to scare you from summer rains.
How you gave up being someone's idea of ugly.
How maybe you were never good at pretending.

I CAN ONLY LOSE YOU SO MANY TIMES

—After Yrsa Daley-Ward

In my dreams we are still small, gorgeous and unfurling,
smoking grass rolled up in notebook paper in the woods
behind our house. You are out of your brain and back
into your body and I am already weeping when morning
breaks. I forgot it was your birthday, but my belly remembers,
all knotted up like it has its own grievances. I move to every
quadrant of the country, looking for the places where we
should be together. Time passes and I wish we looked more alike.
Wish I could look at myself and marvel at how I am you now.
I feel I have betrayed you so many times by continuing to live.
We are both thirty-somethings now, and I realize how little that
means in the absence of babies and mortgages. Atlanta is
sometimes much colder than I'd predicted, and also, you are not
here. And you are not really where you are, either. In my dreams,
I am scrambling after you, always, hoping you'll take me with
you. When I awake, it is always tomorrow—never yesterday like
I'd hoped.

TENDERHEART

Legally,
I am a man now—
according to the Georgia Department
of Driving Services
It feels surreal,
three decades later
and my paperwork no longer lyin' on me
I think I am supposed to feel
like the truth now
I think my driver's license
is a transgender death certificate

This is made complicated
by the fact that I refuse
to eulogize the Black girl,
disappeared by my surgeon
so good that it's almost like
she was never here

This is not a death
Me and that imaginary girl are just
on the run together
Hiding under sunglasses
and too-large hoodies
and trying not to turn our heads
when someone calls us by our old names

It's funny how the world
only searches for missing black girls
after they've confessed
that they never really were girls
just *Black* and *missing*

Perfect in their unwillingness
to be what the world said
what a nigga said
what I said yesterday because
I reserve the right to change my mind–
change my hair and
pop my shit

Rewrite my name over
and over and over
with different letters
until it starts looking right
make you memorize every new spelling,
and then forget them all
if I say so

And maybe today I am a man–
yesterday a Black girl
and while I'm asleep,
I'm nothing but a pyre of 'almosts'
and 'never agains'
The sparks
between my synapses
threaten to catch ablaze
and engulf every version
of the person that I performed today

The first time
I swim in a lake after top surgery,
chest bared to the wild
like twenty years prior
I register
that I am topless and tasty
and terrified
I am torn open

and suddenly so much taller
I get a mosquito bite
just above my nipple
and for some reason
this feels like a gift to me

Afterwards my sister's friend
and I laugh about the blood tax
for wanting to go shirtless in public
I tell her how scary it was
And how absolutely thrilling
I wonder if I'll ever strip myself
without a moment's hesitation
Toss my shirt to the ground
and run for water

She says
yeah, isn't it funny
how they make it all about the body
Being in the *wrong* body
Needing to change your body
Like,
I'm sure you thought your chest
was the thing that was
always holding you back,
and now you realize
it was the shame

MY PULSE, THE UNRELIABLE NARRATOR

again, a boy is in my body

you know it by the way i cannot meet your eyes

i feel his hands where your hands are

and before i can stop it, i am floating above us and you are

holding what's left of the breath

in my boy-broken body

we do this nearly every night

you, a boy, not body-breaker

me, a body

we train ourselves to stay in the pain that is this moment

hoping that i become unbroken

and can see you for your beauty—

not the boy in your body,

and all of the things he could do to mine

in truth, you are a reason i give myself

you are focal to this story and how it ends

let my brain tell it, i am broken

let my pulse have a turn: i've never been more excited

i can be dangerous for you, i have recently decided

might fuck around

and let your love crack me wide open

COUSINS

Growing up Black,
with roots in the South,
means...you 'got a lot of cousins.

· There's the *favorite* cousin,
who always felt more like a big brother

· The *bougie* cousins
who always got on that new shit

· The *hood* cousins
who taught you how to fight

· The *good* cousins
who went to college on scholarship

And the *play* cousins.
Perhaps the most important category:
Your daddy's best friend's daughter
Your homeboy from around the way
that taught you everything you needed to know in this life.
Black folks know to draw the family tree so *big*, and *wide*,
that it has room enough
to encompass anybody that you've ever loved.

So, when you ask me how I can *care so much*,
about someone I don't share blood with,
someone who doesn't share my last name,
the answer is simple:

that's my cousin.

And you might be my play-cousin,
but I don't *play* about you.

I'll call out your name,
but it's been a while,
so check me if I mispronounce it.

¡Viva Viva Tortuguita!
Viva la revolución!

Viva whatever it is
that will keep the air
in my lungs, and yours.

Pull over in Williamsburg, Virginia
for a brown man
on the side of the highway—
his weary thumb outstretched.
Disregard anything I've ever been told
about the danger of men
who look like me.

Same fire, raining on Gaza,
been ringin' off on the east side.
ringin' in my ears
ever since I was a kid
and learned that sirens
didn't mean that help was on the way.
Same fruit, swingin' strange like
loquats, and lush ivy brush.

"Why did you stop for me?" asks Waj
"We gotta stick together," I say.

I don't care from where
you got your brown skin.
We stickin' like brown mud;
like fistfuls of Black cake.
We stickin' like we been stuck,
like we don't know no better.
Like we got the same *short end of the stick*
but we can hold them together.
Like, we in this for the long haul
so pack up all your shit
like I pulled up in the U-Haul—
like *"hop in loser,*
we finna get free today!"

Y'all tweaked if y'all think
my ancestors' wildest dream
was for me to be able to vote
for genocide
keep ignoring homicide
Trans-femicide
I'm not an *activist*
I'm just Black and tired,
so I act like this.
I'm *really* like this.

I promise you,
I would stop for you too—
wallahi.

If they take the Weelaunee,
I promise you:
I will bear witness,
I will not look away,
There is no tomorrow

that I will accept,
that doesn't have you in it.

I will keep your dreams,
hold your hands,
read your poems,
shed tears for you like,
you my little kinfolk
Like "*Yeah,*
you can call me your cousin,
cousin."
From the river to the sea.

HOW I KNOW YOU LOVE ME

I am not a recipe
for your hands or their undoing
you are mine in a way not reliant
on bodies
or borders

There is nothing quite as exotic
or erotic
as the aftercare
& I can wear my bonnet around you

I confess
that I never learned to skip double-dutch
my body don't move like that
no god-given snap, click
tap skip tap
& still,
we make this beat drop
spectral, electrical
eat down, as the babies say

You, a bit of a fabulist
every day, a new favorite thing to share
an incisor, my furrowed brow,
a rougue mustache hair

I know you love me
because you ask me to model
my new shirt
down the catwalk of our dining room
mouth agape
like it's Parisian Fashion Week

& at the slightest hint
of uncertainty from me
you stomp your feet thunderously
pull my hands from my face
& insist
'don't you play me cheap, darling–
let it be glorious'

GRIEF COMPOSITE I.

–*A Golden Shovel After Danez Smith's* Tonight, in Oakland

'It's not giving what it's supposed to give'
you say in your butch-queeniest cadence, laughing and launching your phone at me.
And I don't expect to never see you again, because storm clouds don't always mean rain.
I don't remember stopping to hug you before dashing out into the night or
if I did hug you, it didn't give what it needed to give.
Now, it feels like there are so many different versions of me:
the one whom you would lovingly refer to as honey,
furrowed brow, and tea mug perched like a paid actor, you'd drawl out a thick *'oh dear'*
and tickled, I'd embellish every word until you'd exclaim *'oh my lord!'*
Then, there is the me who ignored every sign, the
one looking upwards and cursing you out now, pretending you are the full black sky
Sure, no one ever knows how long any of us has
But that we'd at least Joan one another for newly graying temples had always felt like a given
There is the me who doesn't know how to be *me* without *us*
There is the one who'd said only one word when they'd called and told me: ***no!***
There is the me that pushes small paper boats into brown river water
covered in words I can't say to you, or anyone, like how enormous this
crater in me feels, or how many times you've broken my heart this year.

Strangers sometimes catch a stray on my worst days when I
glimpse a you-shaped imposter while walking down the street, or out a window on my bus ride.
I am quick to bare my teeth and growl low and throatily, my
façade cracking only as I approach my apartment and see your purple-and-yellow bike,
rusting, still tethered to my gate where you left it on the way to
heaven. Is there a ballroom up there? Is there any place for a
couch covered in plastic, like the one your granny left you, where I can tell you about a boy?
I fake-make-face with your stank bougie aunty when I see her around town, and also when
anyone asks me if you left behind a note, or if I
thought you did it because you didn't have a mama or daddy to get
you together. Truth is, whenever you looked into the future, I don't think you saw yourself there.
And it didn't matter how much you knew I was so mad over you. You always did what
you wanted. I just don't understand why we couldn't keep being a 'we'
for just a little bit longer. I wonder if, when I'm older, it'll make
more sense. I hope that something inside of me will
grow to forgive you someday. And it isn't that I don't understand not
wanting to be alive, or alone, or here to see this world continue to be
so cruel. I just didn't expect you to leave before anything truly became beautiful.

SCORPIO KWANSABA

You: sexy, mystery—stealth like a secret
Me: a little afraid of the sting
Still, you skitter across my open palm
Trace a path that's all your own
I hold you like a heavy tongue
Follow you into the warm broken earth
Follow you into the wide open sky

WORLDS KWANSABA

I will never say I regret it
I can't, I don't—this seismic event
How many little worlds birthed this one?
Gifted you hands and me this mouth
and even this beating heart to break
This time, we're ships in the night
In the next life, we'll see morning

DARK MATTER[7]

There is no wrong way to be a gay Black girl.
Butch bois and golden dyke mouths spit glitter and even
the ones who never really were jazzy or sassy or
rascally can become legitimized between the knees of straight
girls and elsewise. I don't know if I can still speak for us.
Or them. Damn these pronouns and all their dark matter.
Damn every straight girl who made me feel like I didn't matter.
I can hardly deny that I miss being a girl,
Even if I never really was one. But I know how much it means to us,
naming things and all that, binaries and all that. Feeling right and good and even.
I've come out as so many different things, I can't keep my words straight,
back before I was jazzy or sassy or rascally or
a boy or depressed. All the gay Black girls I grew up with look happier now. Or
maybe just they're better at pretending . Matter
of fact, maybe they're just on the straight
and narrow thing because stud was once prison slang and a gay Black girl
looks like a grown man under blue lights. But I'mma even
up the score. Get our lick back. I know I can protect us.
I'm not afraid to spit glitter or spit venom or step behind us.
Pull up behind you mask off, like pre-covid or,
plastic surgeon, mask on, and cut your shit off like they did mine. Even

trans bois can be dyke matter–I mean dark matter.
Keep a strap on us like a gay black girl.
I've never been the violent type. But I'mma always keep my niggas straight.
I look back on my life and try to keep the facts straight.
How I decided to slut out a type of joy that was never meant for us.
How I decided that I couldn't spend the rest of my life pretending to be a girl.
Even though I love gay black girls and I'm really not either or,
just dark matter. A little jazzy and sassy and rascally and I matter.
I've had to learn how to quiet my rage and get on my knees and get even.
I'd like to think that I am becoming better, even
though I can't think of anything better than a Black girl, gay or straight.
So maybe not better, maybe just different, a dark matter
man, girl. A little jazzy butch queen in golden light. A little light for us.
I feel divinely lucky to live out the rest of my days as a soft boy or
whatever they will call me in 30 years. Maybe a retired gay black girl.
I will always remember what it was like growing up gay, black, and girl.
What it meant to us to matter, if only to each other or
Ourselves. I do not regret the girls who created my boihood. There will always be us.

AND SOMEWHERE, ON AN ALTERNATE TIMELINE

Sonya makes pasta al dente.
The water takes especially long to boil,
but it is well worth it in the end.
The next morning,
she feels keenly renewed for Sunday services.

Trayvon gets a cavity
resulting from his sweet tooth;
He doesn't have Skittles again
until he is sneaking Halloween candy
from his daughter's pumpkin-shaped pail

Ever the mama's boy, a distraught George
forgets to call his mom for Mother's Day.
But when he calls her the day after,
she answers–only slightly annoyed with him.

Breonna buys her son a VR headset,
but he soon loses interest.
The first-person shooter games spike his anxiety,
so they both decide to take up yoga.

Sandra's tire flattens on her way to work.
Once it's fixed, she is too late
for her morning meetings
so she decides to take a mental health day,
the summer breeze billowing through her hair
on the drive back home.

Tamir says grace over the Thanksgiving spread.
Despite having accidentally left

one of his favorite toys
at the park a few days earlier,
he is grinning from ear to ear
—most thankful he says,
for the love of his family.

After Alton drops a mixtape,
he becomes a hometown hero.
He occasionally drives his nephew
by the old gas station and says,
"That's where I used to hustle CDs."
"What's a CD?" his nephew asks.

Philando takes his daughter
on a road trip to look at colleges.
He FaceTime's his wife from the hotel,
saying their daughter is forcing him
to learn TikTok dances.
The three of them belly laugh.

Tony has top surgery,
and afterwards, he and his father
get matching chest tattoos to celebrate.
They both say "McDade Men"
in bold, black letters.

Botham gets a promotion at work
and jokes that his best friend
should take him out for drinks.
I'll do you one better, his friend says,
already reaching for the keys
—let's go get some ice cream.

WHAT I KNOW NOW

–A Golden Shovel After Ada Limon's What I Didn't Know Before

It was a small kind thing when
you said, "This pain could be anything—why wouldn't we
make it into your happy ending?" True, our years saw
plenty of coarse exchanges. Miraculously, each
left us both more in love with the other.
It was never about the ending, or what
was clearly the zenith of two unremarkable selves. It was
everything before, after, and between.

BRICKS

I hope all my books are banned books,
like, so contraband
they start trappin' them out the bando—
people fiendin' for my words with such fervor
clawing at the door for just one more taste
someone keeps the lookout
to make sure *twelve* don't see the weight:
tiny baggies filled with poem scraps
pushed out from every corner

I hope my books become
so obscure
that someone's biggest flex
is telling you they've read me
and then you search for my Wikipedia page
and all it says is
-Black
-queer
-longtime resident of the south
-93 'til infinity

I hope white people hate my shit
try to say it means *nothing* in the daylight
feel so raw and dirty
sneaking peaks on the dark web
face a hot mess of flush;
I hope they slam their laptops shut
when they hear footsteps approaching
hang their heads with shame
and spend the rest of their lives wondering
how much they missed out on

I hope they outlaw my books

And then drag queens read them to toddlers
on the front steps of the capitol
I hope there are no front steps
of the capitol
Because I hope the empire falls
I hope a trans woman throws the first brick
And I hope a page ripped from one of my books
is attached to it

I hope, one day, I meet a genocide survivor
all grown up, despite all odds
And they tell me
they know all about my books
And I'll gasp
and ask them how my poems made it to Palestine
Through the whisper network, they'll say
We mixed them with Arabic
and by the time they reached us
they already had French
Haitian Creole and
Swahili in them too

I hope my books are too heady for the Pulitzer
I hope my books get down on the down-low
I hope their registration expires
I hope my books live in infamy
I hope my books turn into history books
buried somewhere long forgotten
only to be dug up
in two hundred years
by whoever is still left on this rock

And they read them
and they cry
and they wonder what made me write these words

and what type of world we were living in
where people banned books
and then they take my books
toss them into a pit
pour one out for an ancestor
and then they burn them for warmth

ENDNOTES

1 *Transitory* originally appeared in issue twelve of Twyckenham Notes, an online literary journal. Brandon Teena was a gender-nonconforming person who was raped and murdered in Humboldt, Nebraska, in 1993. His life and death were the subject of the critically acclaimed film *Boys Don't Cry*.

2 *How to Survive A G*rlhood* is a found poem assembled from quotes in a series of oral histories conducted for my dissertation research. Quotations were sourced from conversations with the following interlocutors: Maxx Maxwell, Jacquilyn (Jack) Simmons, Dr. LaTreese Denson, Tyson Marzouq, Tyler Dykes, Keena (KB) Blythe, Kabir Amari Gilyard, Bri Bolden, and Sir Lex.

3 *Chest Binder Bliss // Top Surgery Blues* is both a contrapuntal and a concrete poem. Contrapuntal poems are designed to be read in more than one direction (in this case, vertically on both the left and right sides through the merging point, as well as altogether from left to right). Concrete poems take on the physical shape of their topic. This poem, inspired by the chest dysphoria and euphoria I experienced before and after my gender affirmation surgery in December 2021, was first published in *Room Magazine*.

4 Inspired by Kwanzaa in the mid-1990s, Eugene Redmond invented the Kwansaba form: seven lines of seven syllables each, comprised of words with seven or fewer letters. The form was created as praise poems celebrating the Black experience.

5 *Masculinity & Femininity* is a blackout poem created using text from Beth L. Bailey's *From Front Porch to Back Seat: Courtship in Twentieth-Century America.*

6 To create this Blackout poem, I used a 2020 article from Essence.com, written by Breanna Edwards, as source material. The article chronicles the police murder of a Black trans man, Tony McDade, a mere two days after the widely publicized and protested police murder of George Floyd. Compared to the coverage of Floyd's killing at the hands of Minnesota police, McDade's death was relatively absent from mainstream media coverage, and in initial reports, he was frequently misgendered.

7 *Dark Matter* is a sestina, a poetic form featuring thirty-nine lines (six stanzas plus an envoi) written in a set alternating end-word pattern. This poem was originally published in Scalawag Magazine, a social justice–oriented publication centered on the South.

ACKNOWLEDGMENTS

Each of these poems is its own small universe, carrying a fragment of the larger story I've been trying to tell—about grief and becoming, about intimacy, memory, love in its most radical iterations, and the long pursuit of liberation. I'm deeply grateful to every editor, journal, and publication that welcomed these pieces into their own archives and offered them space to live for the first time.

Amorphaville BIPOC Anthology
- "Parable of the Innocent, or black trans-boi roadmap"
- "Honest Bodies Cento"

Beestung
- "Glory Days"

Birdcoat Quarterly
- "sonnet for the indecisive"

Cathexis Northwest Press
- "you can swim underwater, just don't breathe in"

Fruitslice | A Queer Quarterly
- "Self Portrait as Pi"

Hare's Paw Literary Journal
- "What Didn't Happen When We Kissed"

Hooligan Magazine
- "How I Know I Love You"

MAYDAY Magazine
- "the revolution might not be televised"
- "pepper jack"

Mulberry Literary
- "Cousins"

Orca Literary Journal
- "tenderheart"

Pile Press
- "My Pulse, The Unreliable Narrator"

Room Magazine
- "how two depressives manage coexistence"
- "Chest Binder Bliss // Top Surgery Blues"

Sad Girl Diaries
- "requiem for a gone girl"

Sad Girl's Club Literary Blog
- "The Body (in theory)"

Scalawag Magazine
- "How To Survive A G*rlhood"
- "Dark Matter"

South Florida Poetry Journal
- "what men are made of"
- "How I Know You Love Me"

The Blood Pudding
- "night balm quartern"

The Hellbore Press
- "if I must live after Refaat Alareer"
- "tenderheart"

The Moving Force Journal
- "Linguicism"

The Passionfruit Review
- "A.B. Persona Poem – A Golden Shovel After Patricia Smith's 'Always In The Head'"

Twyckenham Notes
- "Transitory"

Voicemail Poems
- "Bricks"
- "After Sula"

WUSSY Magazine, Issue 14
- "stories we tell ourselves"

ABOUT THE AUTHOR

Dr. Kelsey L. Smoot (they/he/Kelz) is a gender theorist, an elective Southerner, a writer, and a poet. His autoethnographic style has become the lens through which he understands and reflects on his experience navigating the US sociopolitical landscape. Currently, Kelz serves as an Assistant Managing Editor at Sundress Publications. They are the winner of the 2021 Sad Girls Club Spring Literary Contest, the 2023 *The Good Life Review* Honeybee Prize, and the Grand Prize Winner of the 2024 Button Poetry Video Contest. Kelz is a Tin House Workshop alum, a Pushcart Prize nominee, a Best of the Net nominee, and a Best New Poets nominee. In addition to *SOULMATE AS A VERB*, he is also the author of two chapbooks: *we was bois together* with CLASH! (An Imprint of Mouthfeel Press) and *Muse*, with Another New Calligraphy.